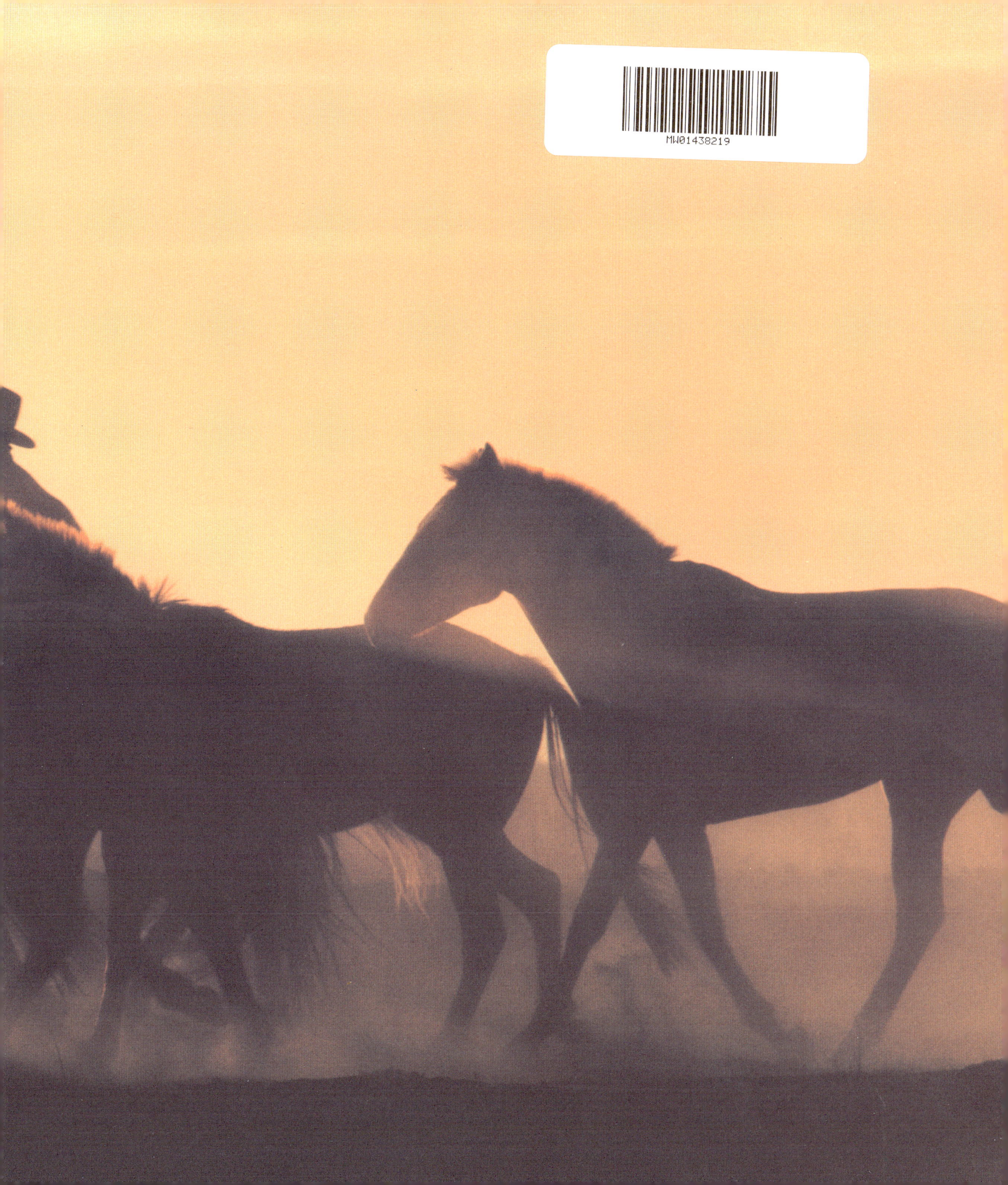

A Taste of the Land

Old Barioolah homestead in far south-west Queensland, built by John Conrick in 1895

Photography..........................Mark Coombe

Poetic description..............Carrie Batzloff

Acknowledgments

This book would not have been possible without the willing help of many of the wonderful people who live on the land. To my father when he was at Waverley Station, the Ellrott family near Rockhampton, Stanbroke Pastoral Company and all the hard-working people at Nappa Merrie Station, David at Nockatunga, the O'Shannessy family on Boodgherree, and Ferret and the shearers, I thank you all very much.

Thanks also to John for all his advice and precision in developing and printing the photos. Extra thanks to Carrie, whose words have brought out the feeling and emotions that I have tried to capture on film.

Of course one does not spend time taking photos in outback Australia without being away from home. Thanks Suellen for your encouragement and tolerance.

Mark Coombe
Rockhampton
1996

Riding at the mob's side

Table of Contents

Preface 4

On the Sheep's Back 5

Muster on the Cooper 14

Faces of the Bush 44

Coastal Collection 54

Lasting Images 66

Preface

Despite the harshness and remoteness of this country, it is the dedication of people living on the land that has made Australia one of the most productive countries on earth. The stockmen, the shearers, the managers, the truckies, the cooks, the women and the children who live their lives on the land they love are often the forgotten ones. They cope daily with the harshness of nature, her floods and her droughts.

They work from dawn till dusk, often hundreds of kilometres from any other civilisation with only their cattle, sheep, horses, their mates and sometimes but rarely their families as companions.

This book is dedicated to all the hard-working people on the land who make Australia such a great nation.

Photos in 'A Taste of the Land' were taken mainly on properties in Central Queensland and in the far south-west of the state. I was raised on cattle stations in Central Queensland and have tried to capture some of the rare moments that make this life on the land what it is.

Many of the images in the book were taken from the back of a horse in hot dusty conditions that don't really favour photography. It does, however, let me get close to the action and capture the atmosphere as felt by a stockman doing his or her job.

I hope you enjoy 'A Taste of the Land'.

Mark Coombe

On the Sheep's Back ...

Awaiting the shearer's blade

Photos in this chapter were taken on Boodgherree Station in far South West Queensland

The road to Boodgherree Station, a dusty red track lined by the occasional Bloodwood tree. Located 80km south of Thargomindah, the station owes its existence to the dedication of the O'Shannessy family.

Water on Boodgherree Station is supplied from three artesian bores and one subartesian bore. Troughs and bore drains distribute this lifeblood to the cattle and sheep that share the property which is in the middle of one of the worst droughts on record.

Hands and wool

Little has changed in Australian shearing sheds in the past 100 years

The Shearer

*For money, not love,
he defies push and shove
of the corporate land.
Instead he dons jeans,
torn 'n' ripped at the seams,
takes shears firm in hand.*

*He begins at first light,
bare knuckles still white
from yesterday's herd.
Steel harness in place,
he'll silently race
till dusk's final word.*

*The heat and the smell,
he knows it too well
is slowing him, but
There's no time to waste—
fame follows the haste
of the cleanest white cut.*

*A simple old life:
no trouble, no strife;
just the sheep and the shed.
Not even the noise
of the shears and the boys
can quieten the dreams in his head.*

The shearer

Overleaf: The Boodgherree shearing shed

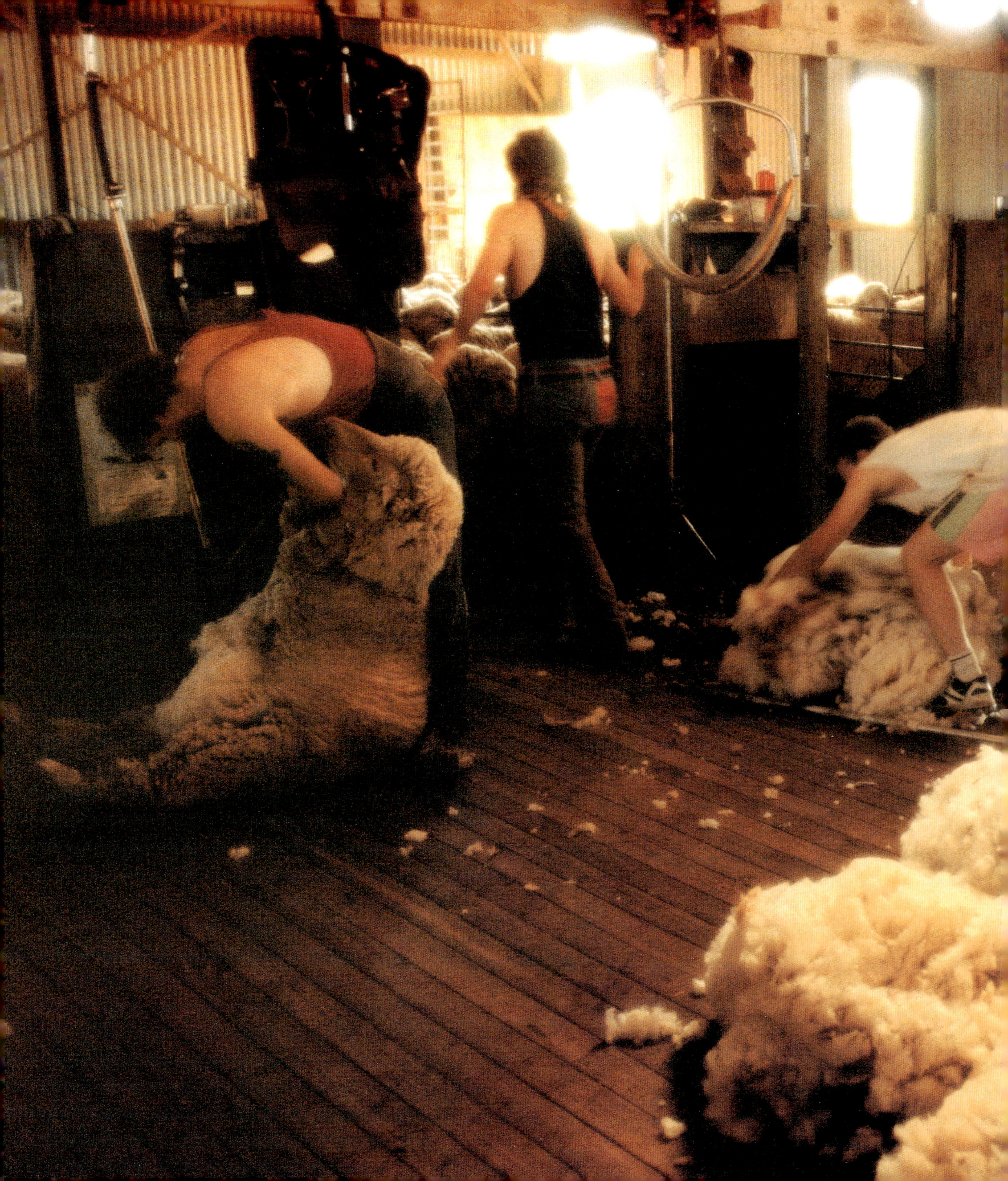

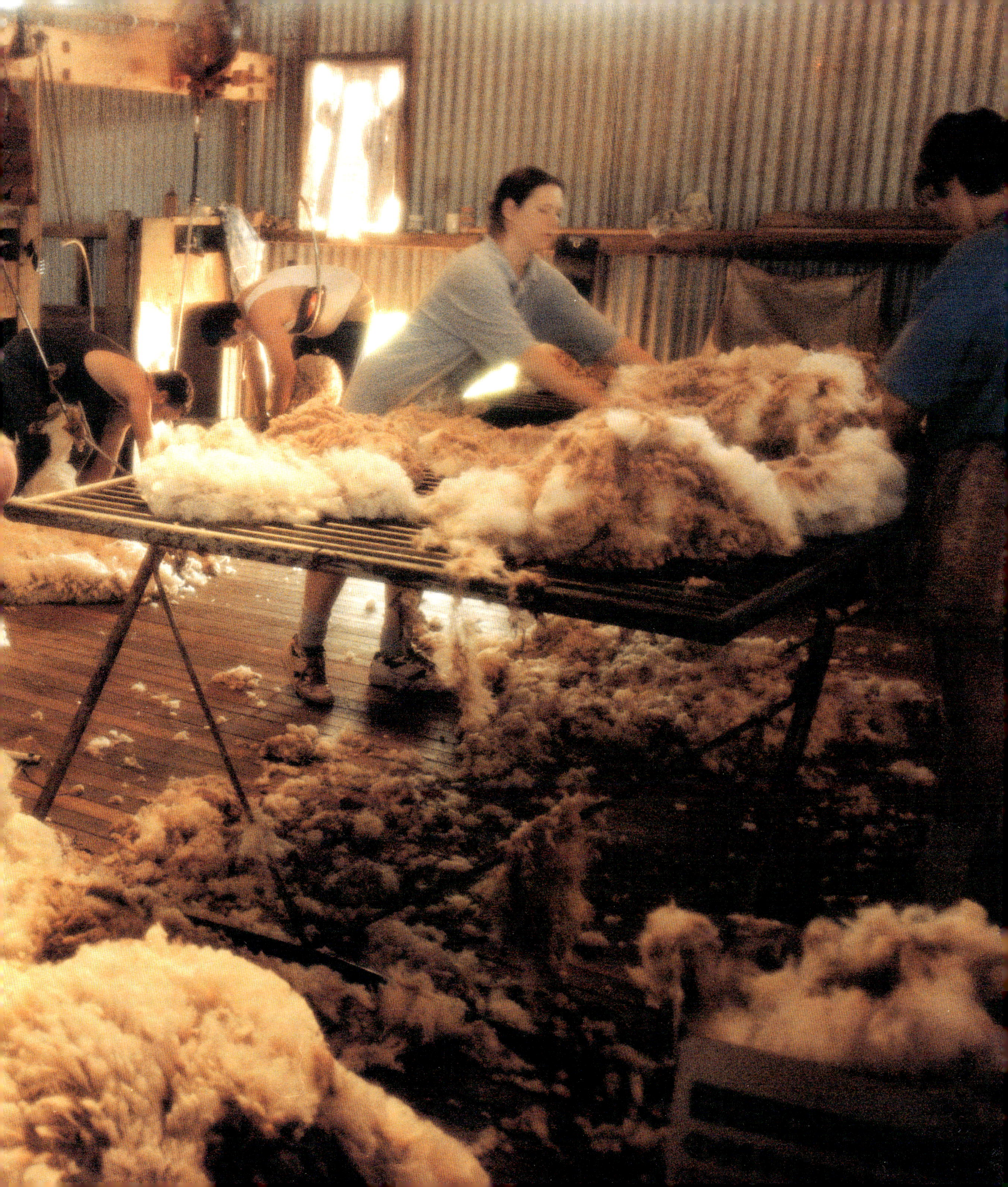

Muster on the Cooper ...

One of the many channels of the Cooper

Muster on the Cooper was photographed on Nappa Merrie Station in south-west Queensland

The delicious taste of sweet water

Stock Camp

First light, moon bright
makes way for eastern sun;
Dry air, no care
for sleep that's been undone.

Fire burns, group yearns
for breakfast to be fed;
Bed rolls, weary souls
prepare for work ahead.

The Essentials

A saddle of soft and comfortable leather;
Jeans blue and stitched for all types of weather;
Boots of raw toughness so they can withstand
the rigours and harshness of life on the land.

Warming up for the day ahead

Taking the horses to water

Time for a smoke

Helicopter pilot and stockman take time to discuss the day ahead

Leading the mob

With about 2000 in the mob, the chopper continuously circles large areas of the paddock bringing cattle to the main mob as it moves from one camp to the next.

Holding up the mob

Drinking opportunities are never missed

Images of the muster ...On the plains

...Through the channels

Overleaf: Channel crossing

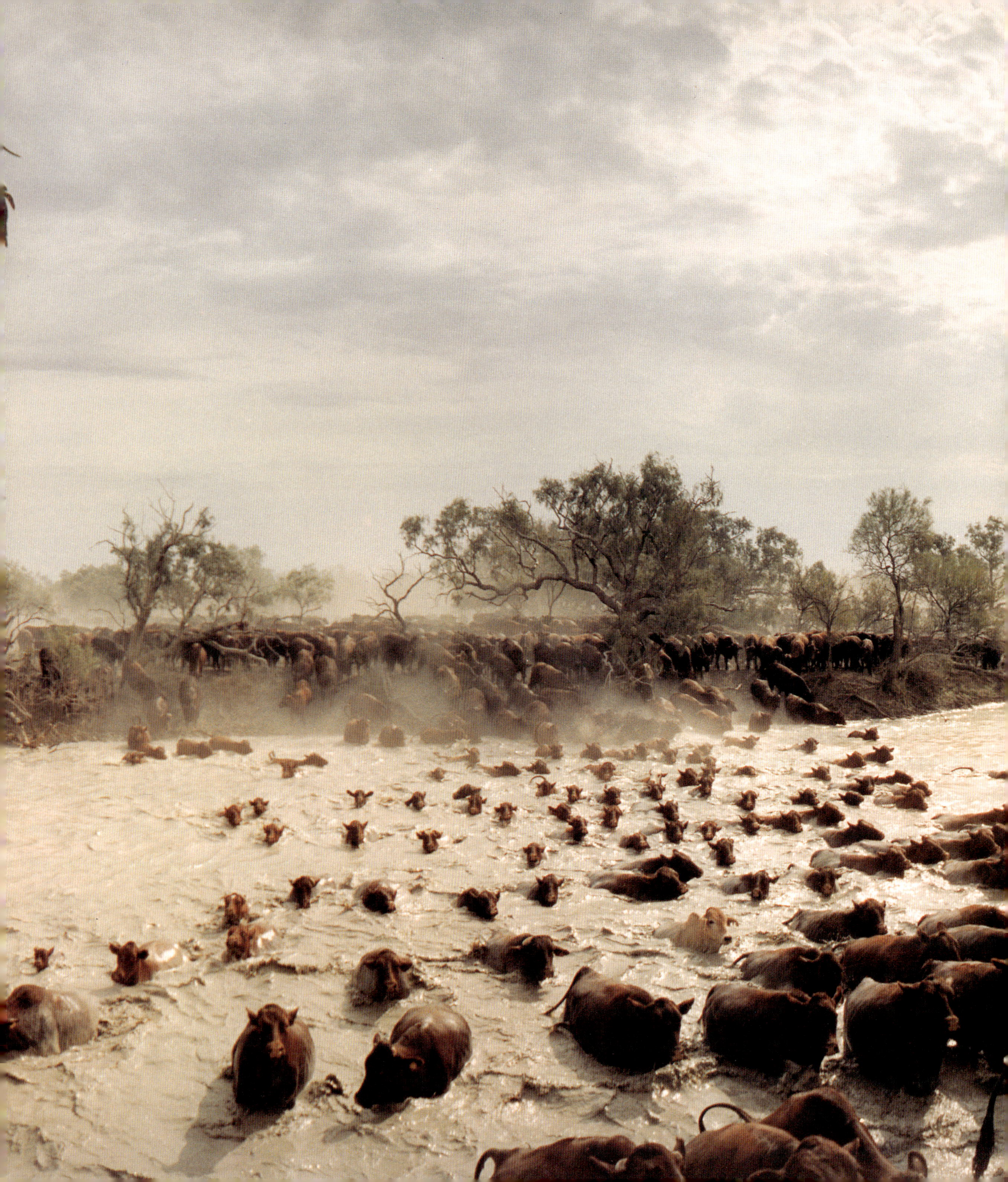

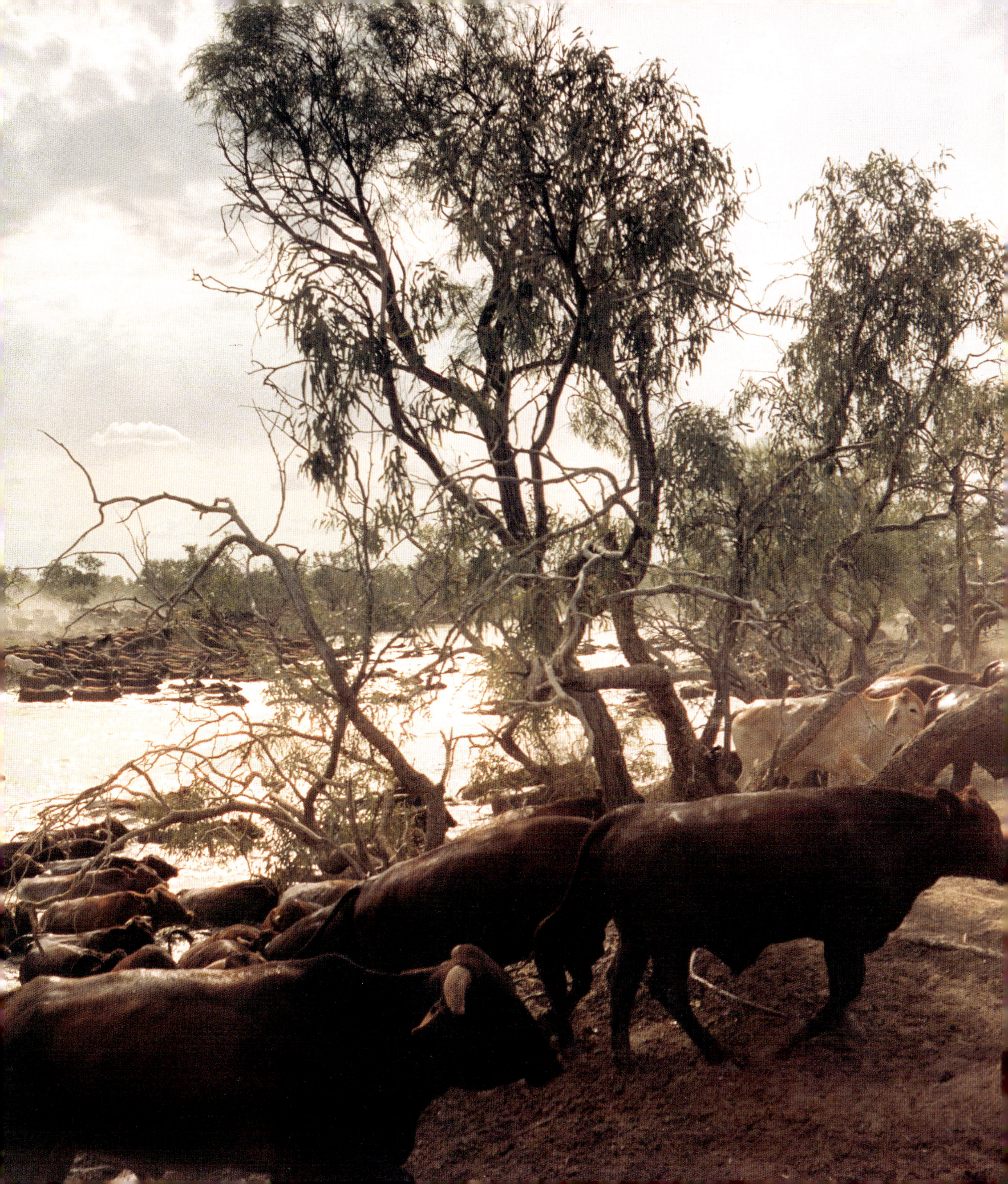

Swimming the channel

Stockmen push in the last of the mob

Prime Santa Gertrudis steers

Waiting for the chopper

*The taste of the land sets dry on my tongue
and stings the parched slits of my eyes.*

*Tis no hearty fare — just hooves running bare
and sending dust clouds to the skies*

Dust storm at Barioolah

Nature's Power

*Stillness grips the empty sky
and slices through the ground;
as slowly from the divots deep
there comes a thunderous sound—*

*Arising from the bellows bold
to tell a fearsome tale;
then just beyond the rolling dune
the sound becomes a wail.*

*The stockman turns a weary head
in time to see his foe
draw life from barren, dusty earth,
raw power from below.*

*A lightning crack tears through the sky;
the wind whips death to life;
and there before the stockman stands
a tower of strength and strife.*

*Too late—the cattle see the storm
and fear takes hold the mob
which turns its back to shield the wrath
and thwart the stockman's job.*

*He does his best to stem the tide
of wayward roaming beasts,
but nature's won this battle grand
—a half day's work at least.*

Overleaf: Dwarfed by the approaching dust storm, cattle make their way to what little protection the few trees will provide.

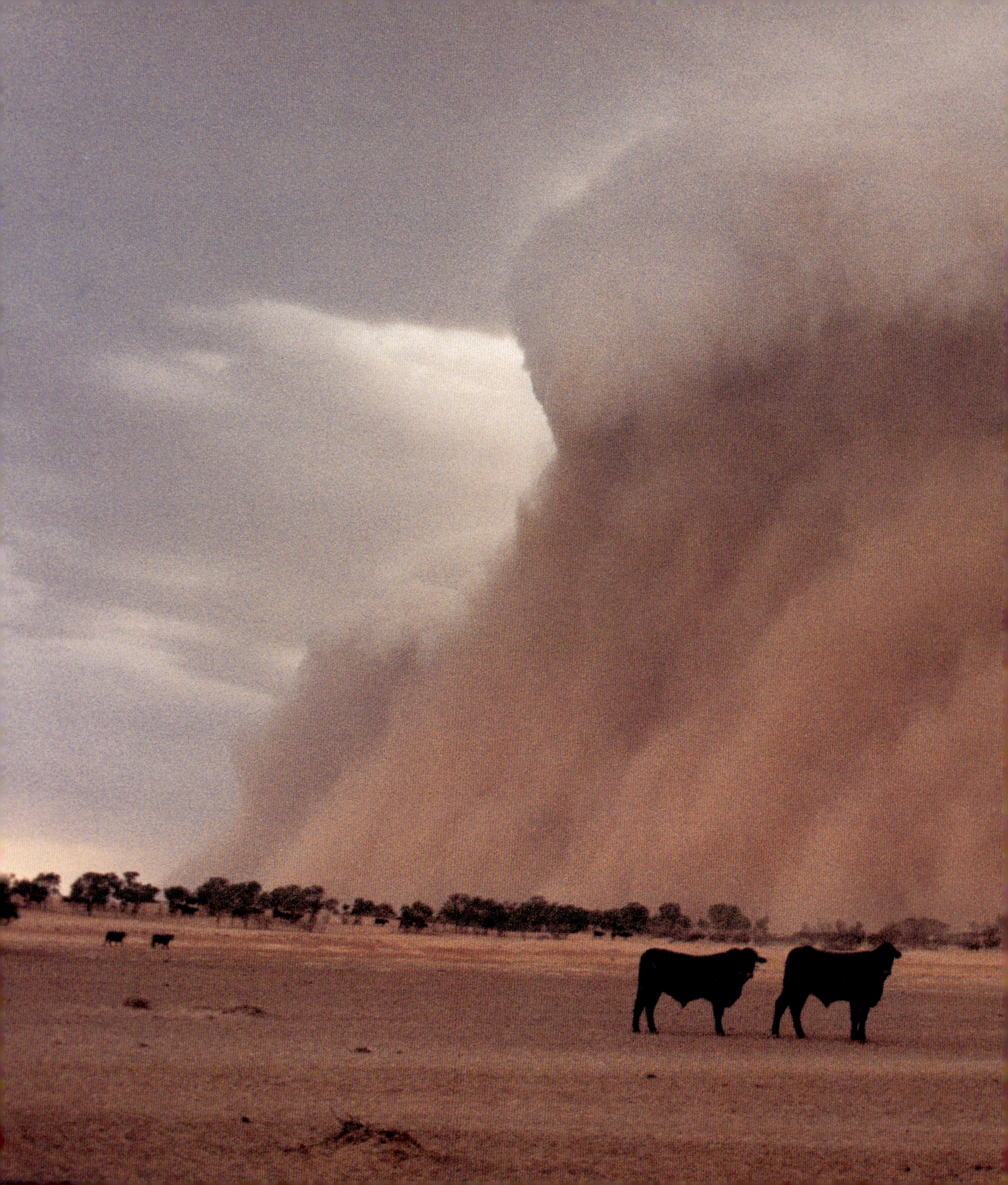

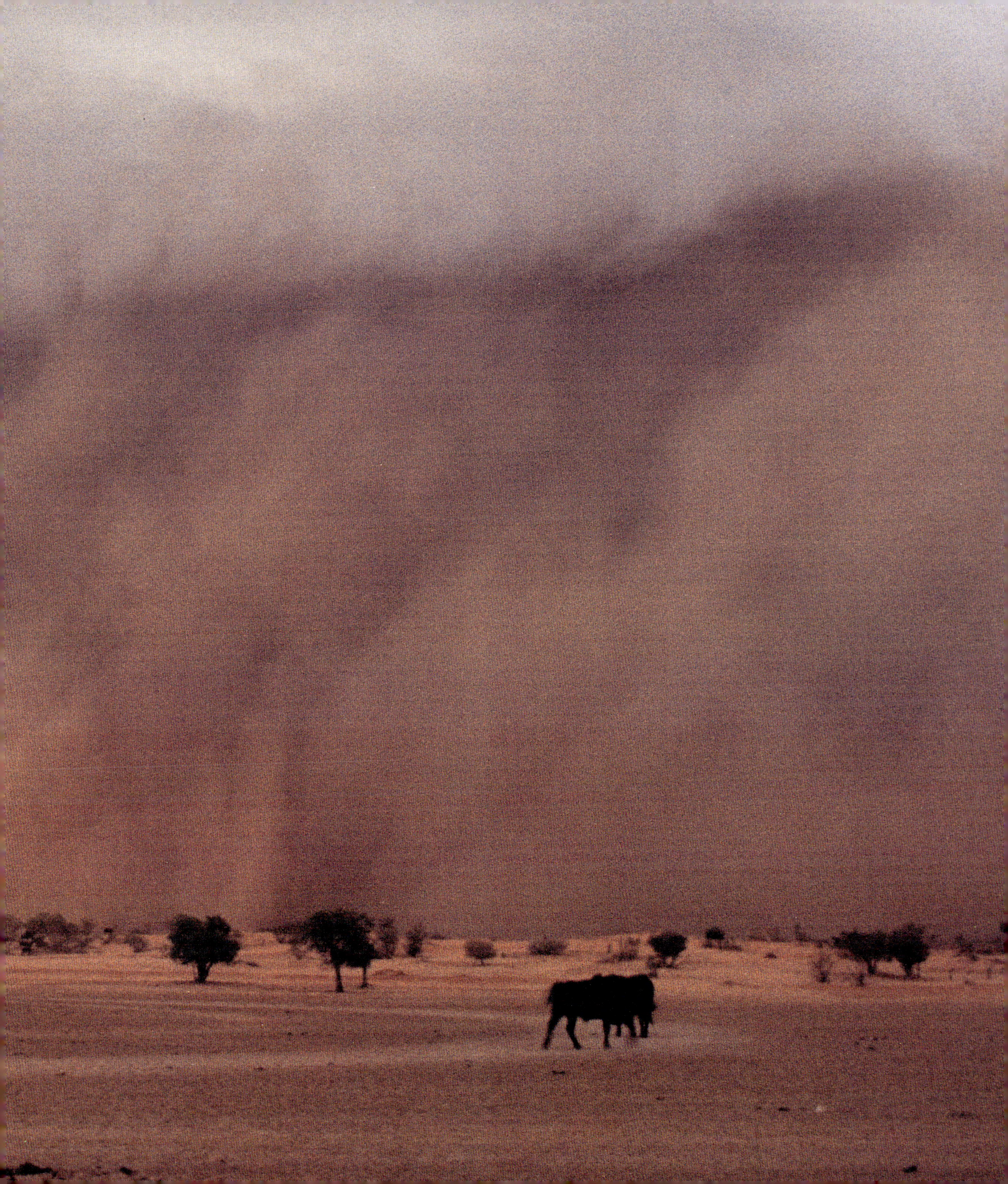

In the yards at last

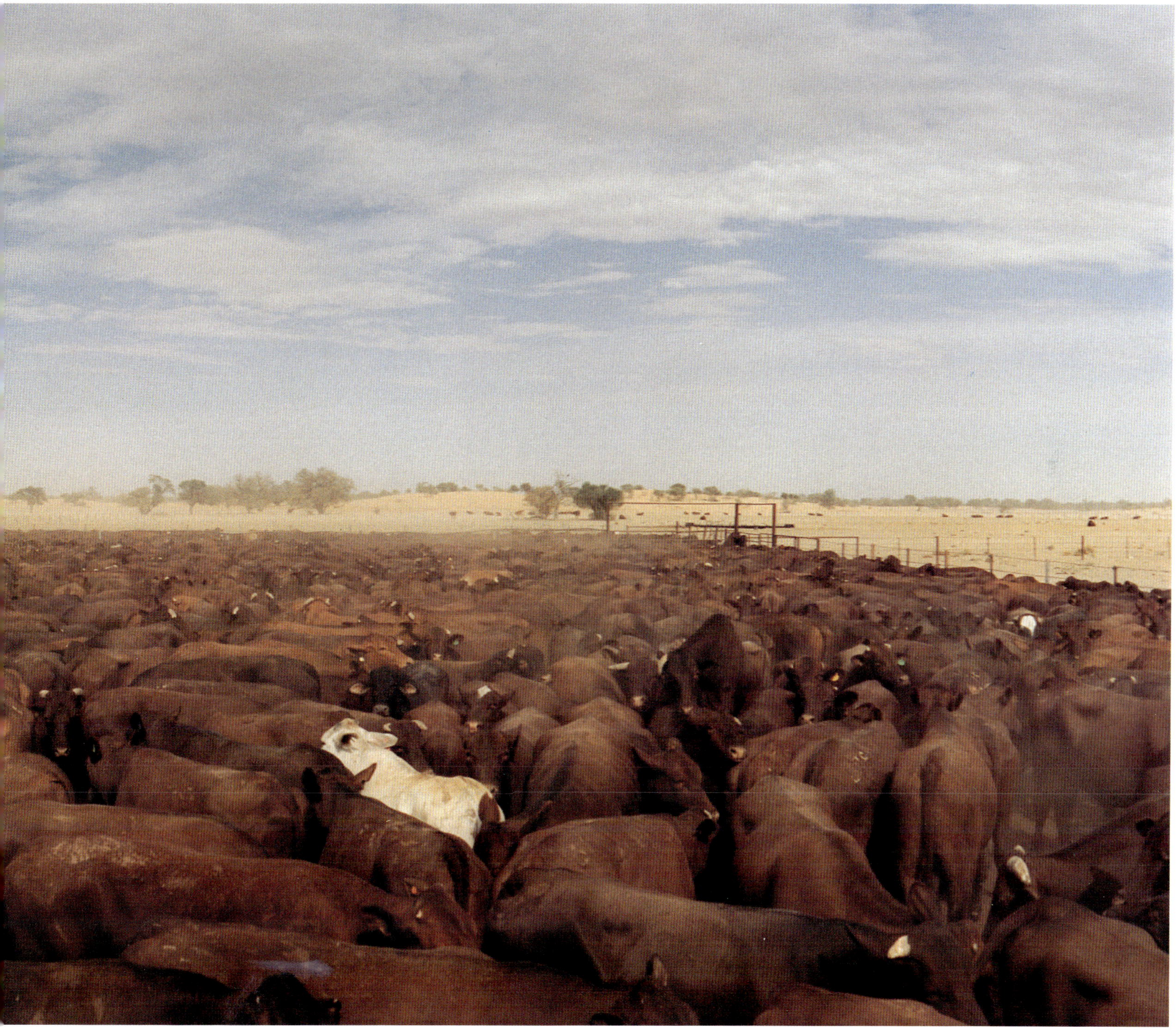

Watering the horses

Cooling down

Faces of the Bush ...

The face of Burke, carved into a tree near the dig tree on the banks of the Cooper by John Dick in 1898

Loyalty

Mustering pilot

Ferrett, the head shearer

Tighten the girth

Clean the shears

Companions

The Stockman

*As old as time itself,
the stockman of the outback
is tough as hardened leather;
as dry as thirsty earth…*

*L*oyal, strong and undemanding—
Ours is a simple understanding

*to work as one through days unbroken
and share a language felt not spoken*

Coastal Collection ...

Good times at Roxborough

The coastal collection is made up of photos taken on Central Queensland properties:
Waverley Station, Balallan, Roxborough and Apis Creek

Right: Towering gums of coastal Queensland

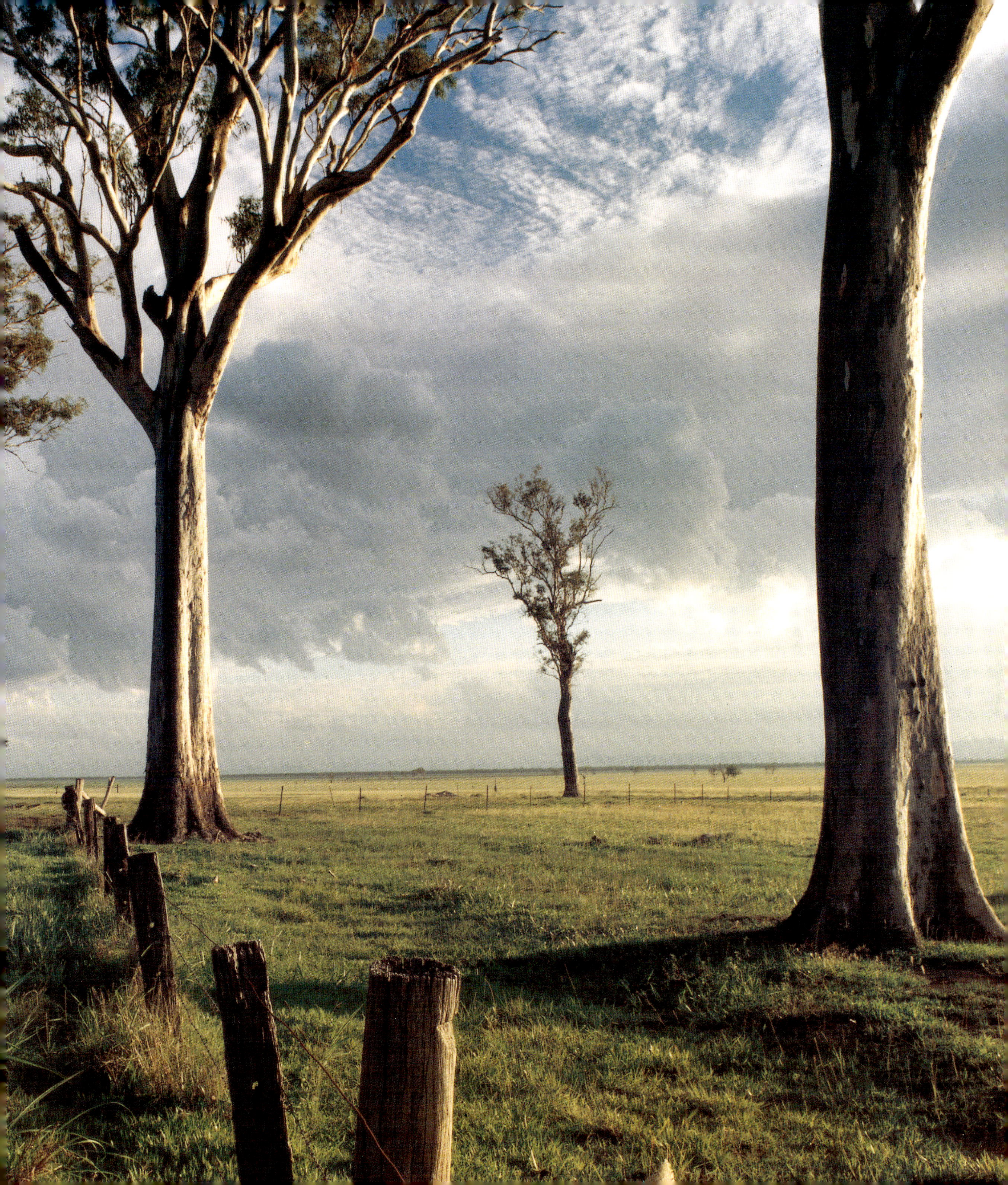

Sunlight and dust

Afternoon light sparkles on the grass

Heading for home

A time for rain

No more the stain of dust and dry
land raped by hot despair;
for heaven's dropped its mother lode
of ample rain to share.

No more the sallow cattle lie
in makeshift dirty graves;
now fat and grand they saunter past
knee-deep in grassy waves.

No more a scene of misery,
of pallide browns and red,
of empty streams and dried-up creeks,
of mulga strangled dead.

Now heavy sags the blackened sky
and swallows up the sun;
its belly full of better times
with still more rain to come.

Overleaf: Rain at Waverley

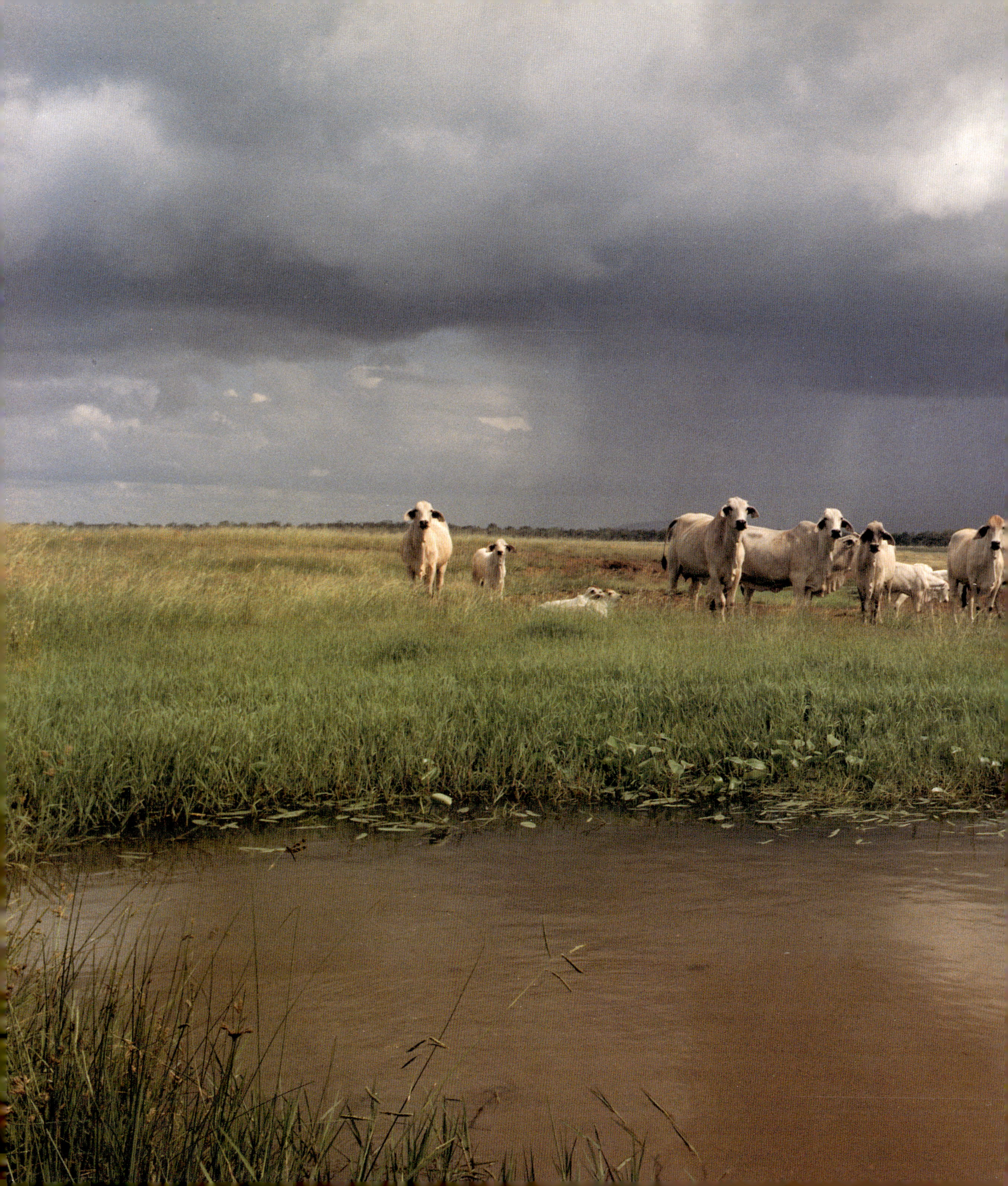

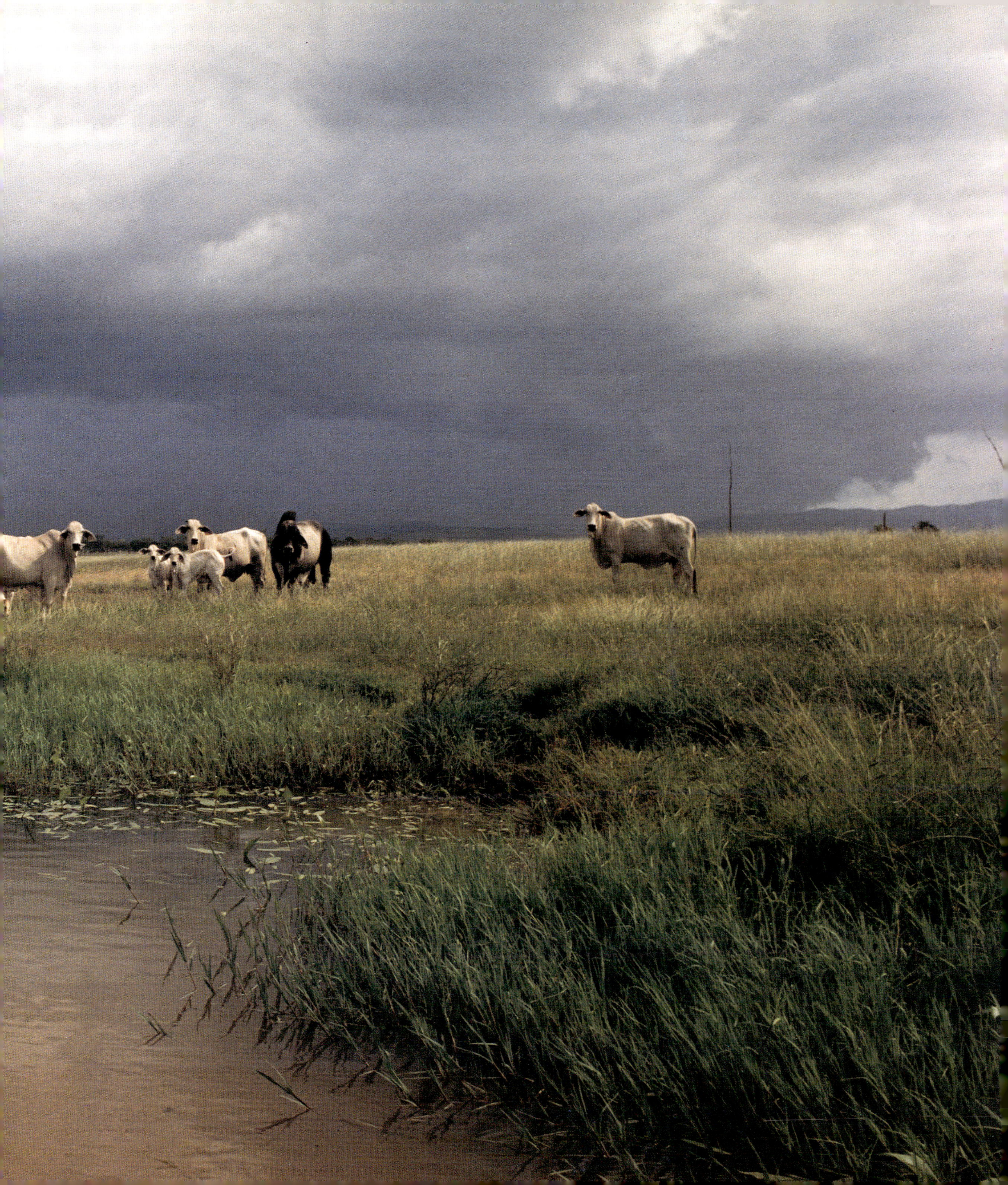

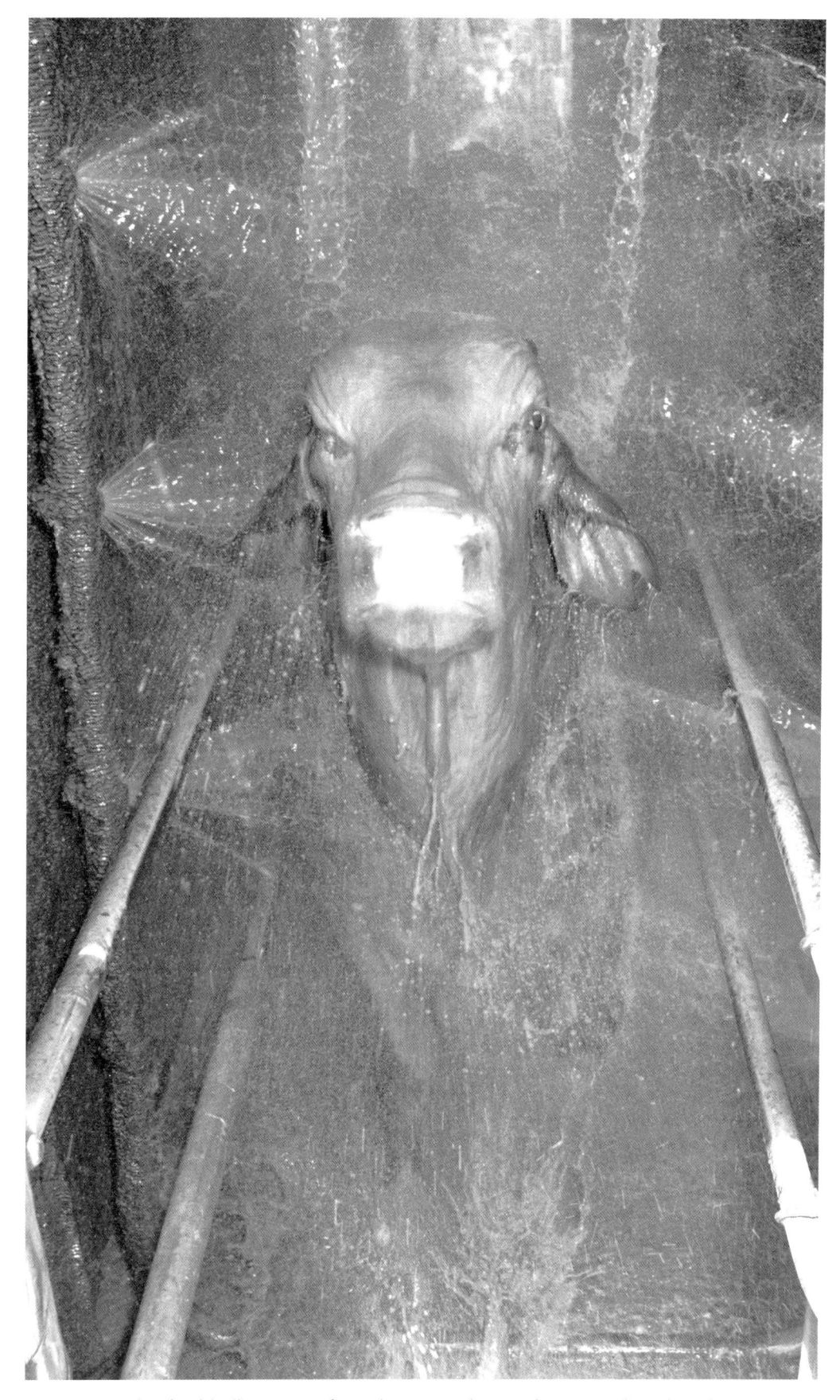

A braford bull emerges from the spray dip used to control cattle ticks

Taking the mob home

The stockman's job

Baby cattle evoke the same strong emotions as do all baby animals. The characteristics of a new calf speculatively viewing the outside world shows a different side to an industry that is known for hard times and heavy work.

Lasting Images ...

Some of the images we see remain with us forever and make Australia such an amazing place

St. Anne's homestead on Nappa Merrie Station, built around 1900

A crack in the parched earth seeps life to a survivor of Australia's droughted land

Roadtrains frequent the very remotest of locations

*F*ew vehicles brave the beaten tracks
which scar the barren land.

*Those that do may not come back —
as rusty shells they stand.*

The struggle for life

The shearer and the sheep

Horses at sunup

Now a permanent part of the outback

Loading cattle onto road trains at Nockatunga for the long journey to Rockhampton

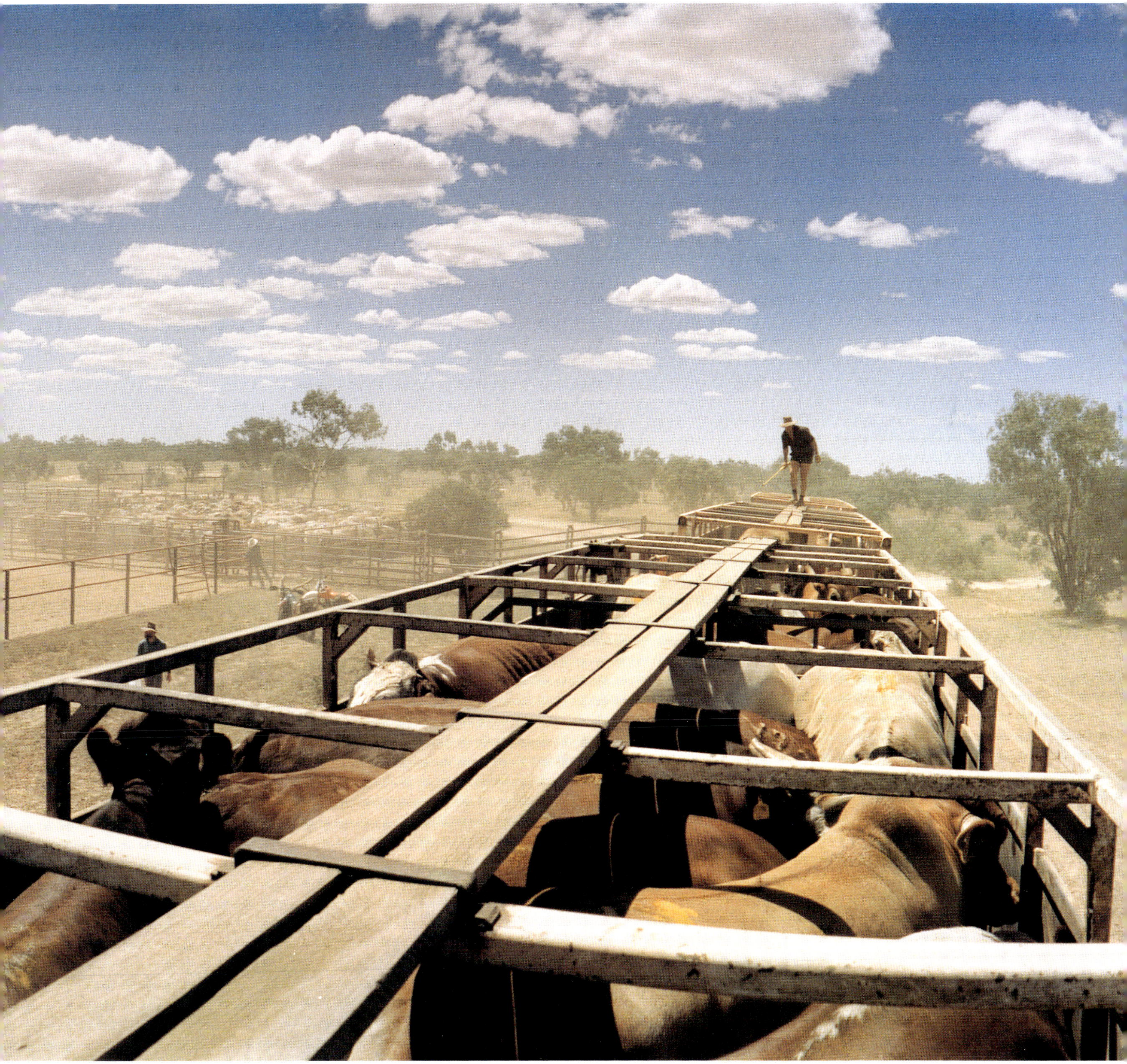

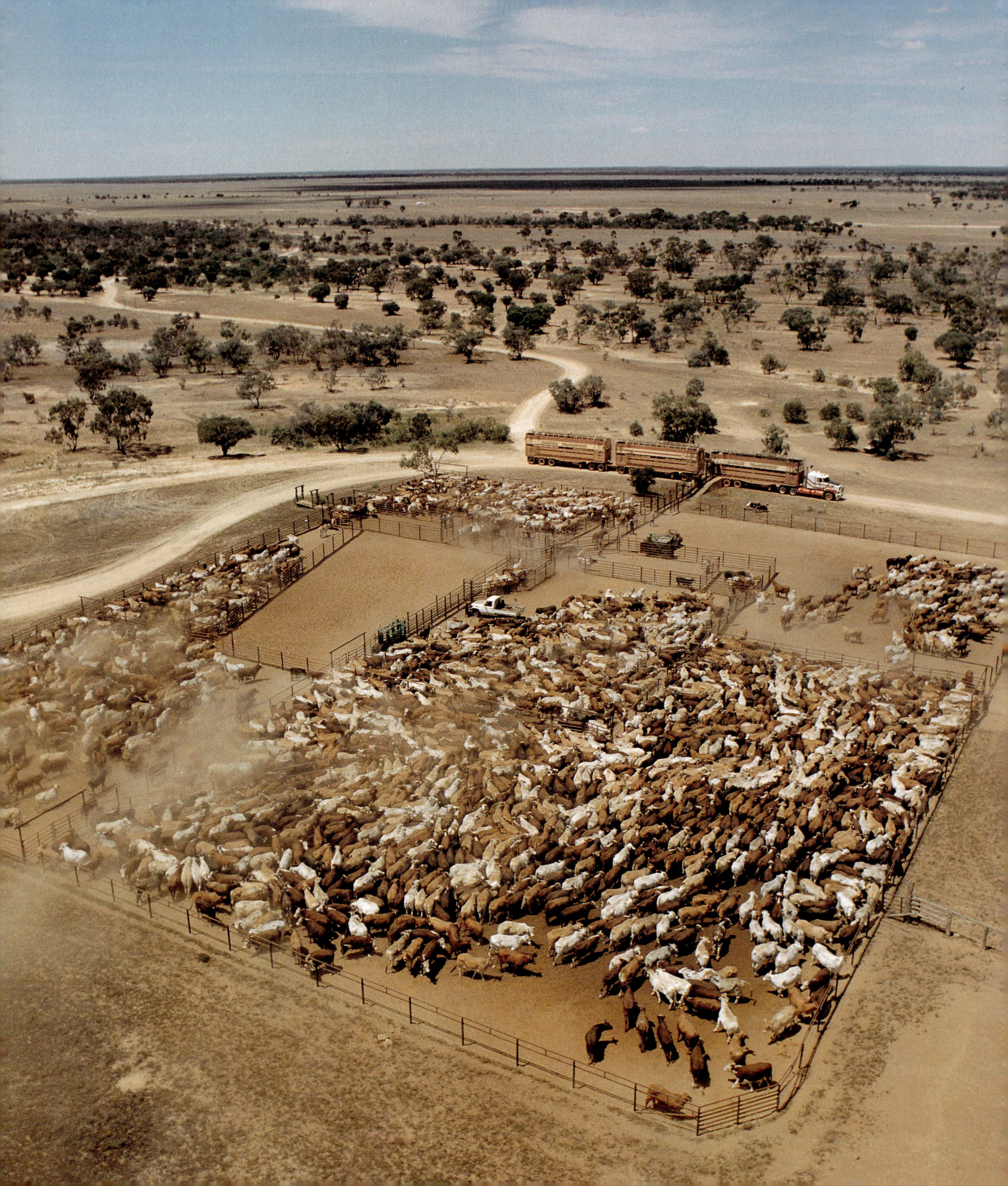

...then it was night

Left: Conbar yards at Nockatunga

A Taste of the Land

ISBN 0646 258680

Pictures and text: Mark Coombe
Poetic description: Carrie Batzloff

© Mark Coombe

First published in 1996 by
    Mark Coombe
    Box 5431 Rockhampton Mail Centre Queensland 4702 Australia

All rights reserved. No part of this publication may be reproduced, stored or transmitted in any form or by any means without the written permission of the publisher.

Typeset by CQPR Media, Rockhampton, Queensland
Printed in Hong Kong by South China Printing Co.

Many of the photographs in this book are available as limited edition photographic prints. For further information contact:
    Mark Coombe
    Box 5431
    Rockhampton Mail Centre
    Queensland 4702 Australia
    (079) 344412

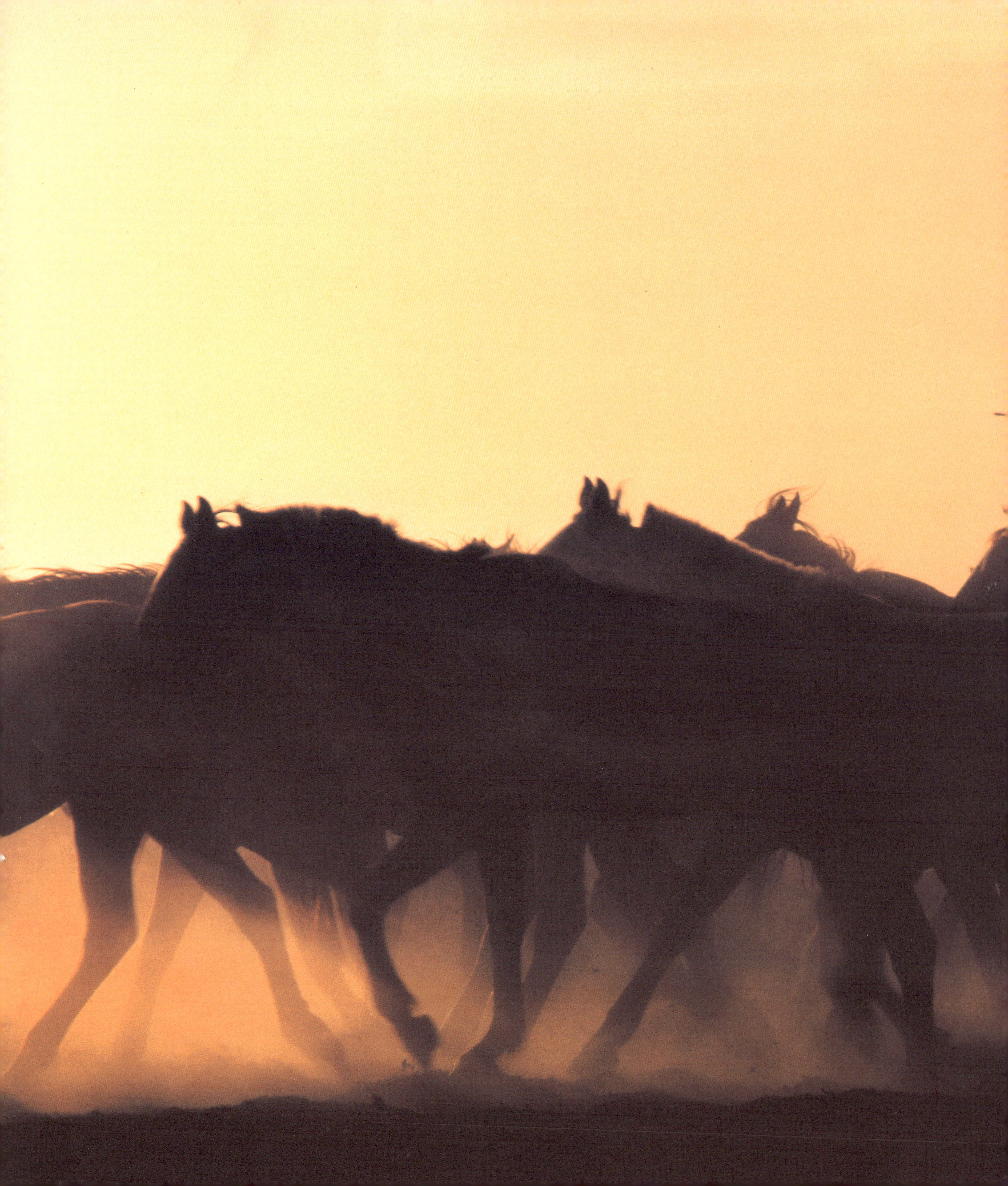